IN RAINBOWS

RADIOHEA_D

© 2007 by Faber Music Ltd
First published by Faber Music Ltd in 2007
3 Queen Square, London WC1N 3AU

Arranged by Olly Weeks
Edited by Lucy Holliday

Artwork by Stanley Donwood + DR TCHOCK
Designed for Faber by Lydia Merrills-Ashcroft

Printed in England by Caligraving Ltd

The text paper used in this publication is a virgin fibre
product that is manufactured in the UK to ISO 14001
standards. The wood fibre used is only sourced from
managed forests using sustainable forestry principles.
This paper is 100% recyclable

ISBN10: 0-571-53117-2
EAN13: 978-0-571-53117-2

To buy Faber Music publications or to find out about the full
range of titles available, please contact your local music
retailer or Faber Music sales enquiries:

Faber Music Ltd, Burnt Mill, Elizabeth Way,
Harlow, CM20 2HX England
Tel: +44(0)1279 82 89 82
Fax: +44(0)1279 82 89 83
sales@fabermusic.com
fabermusic.com

15 STEP

Words and Music by Thomas Yorke, Jonathan Greenwood,
Colin Greenwood, Edward O'Brien and Philip Selway

♩ = 184

Original key down a semitone

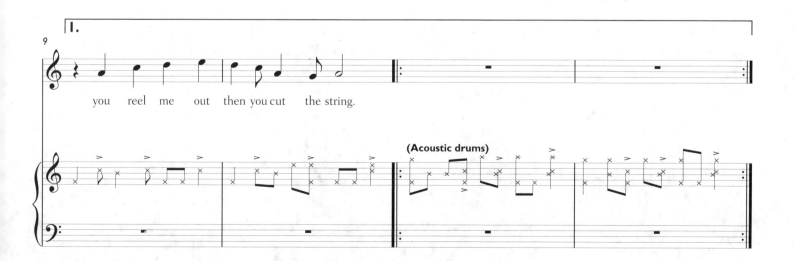

soft_____ as your_____ pil - low._____

D.𝄋 al Coda

Fif-teen steps, then a sheer drop.

(Children shouting)

(Hey!)

Repeat ad lib. to fade

BODYSNATCHERS

Words and Music by Thomas Yorke, Jonathan Greenwood,
Colin Greenwood, Edward O'Brien and Philip Selway

Tune guitar ⑥ = D (lowest string)

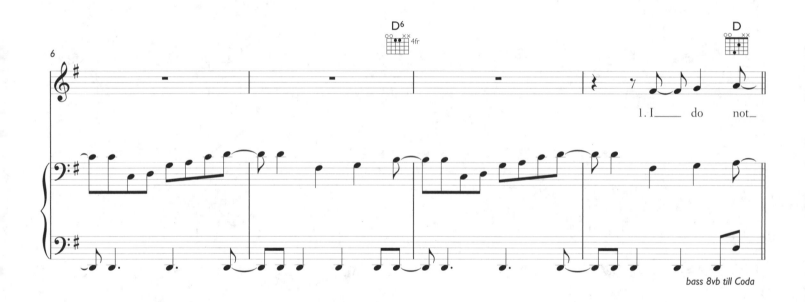

wrapped round my face, on the lines wrapped round my face are for

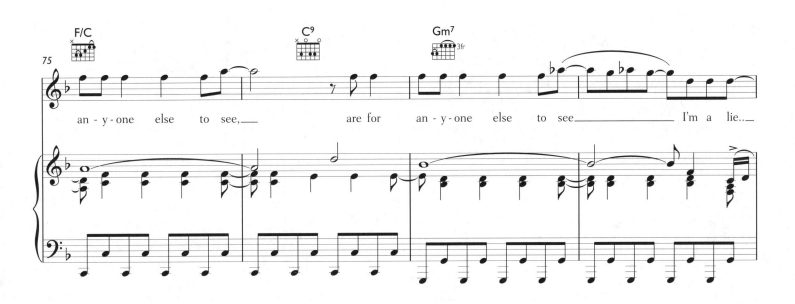

an-y-one else to see, are for an-y-one else to see I'm a lie..

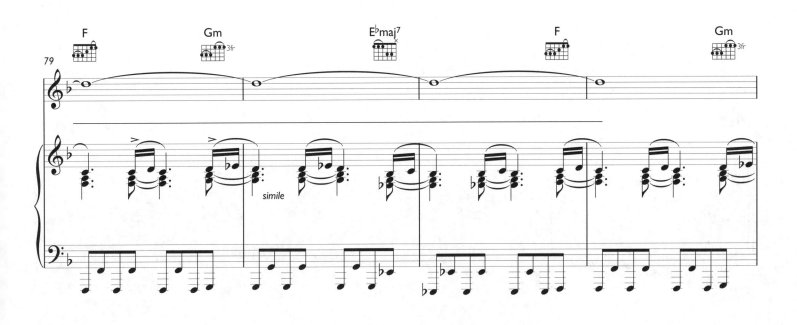

simile

NUDE

**Words and Music by Thomas Yorke, Jonathan Greenwood,
Colin Greenwood, Edward O'Brien and Philip Selway**

Free tempo

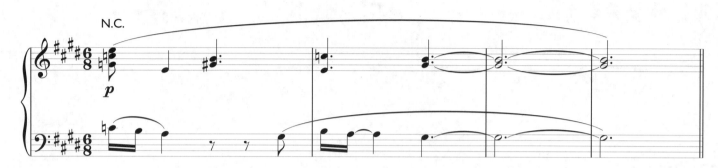

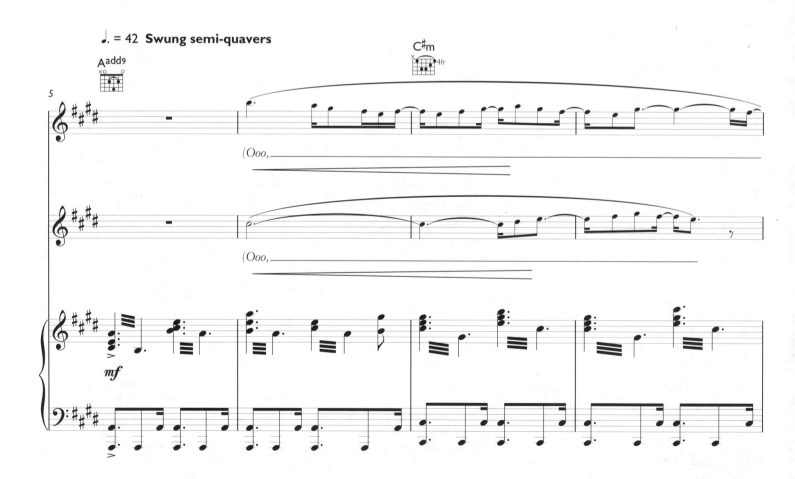

(Ooo,

(Ooo,

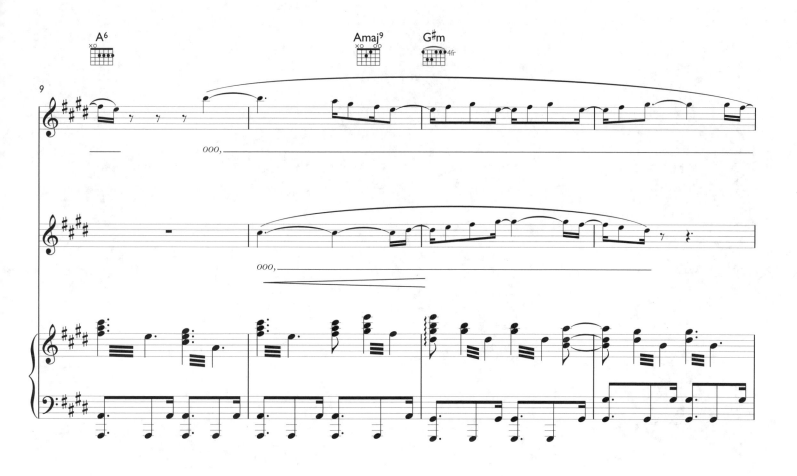

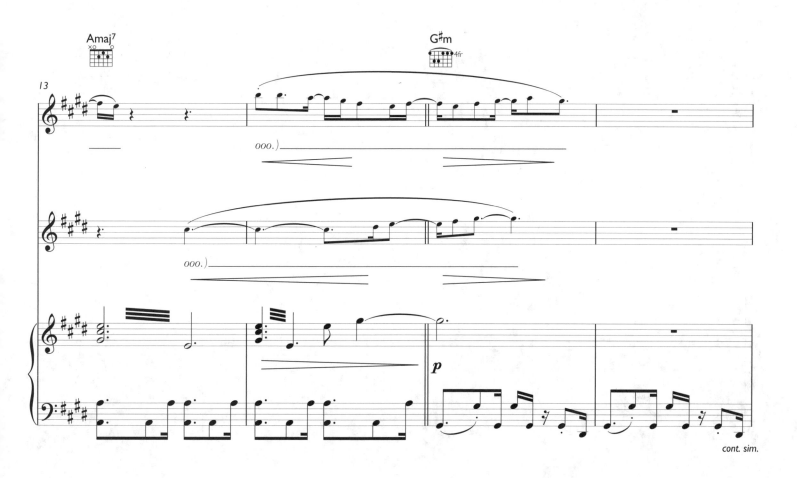

Don't get an-y____ big i - deas.____

They're____ not____ gon-na hap - pen.____

You paint your-self white____ and fill up with noise

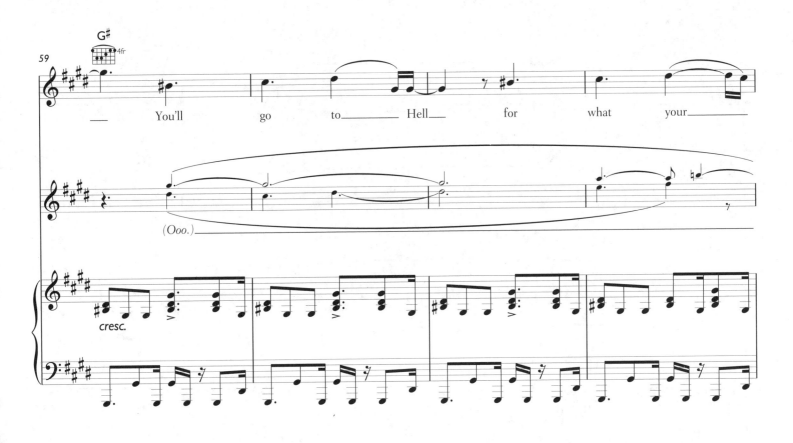

You'll go to Hell for what your
(Ooo.)

dir - ty mind is think - ing. (Ooo,

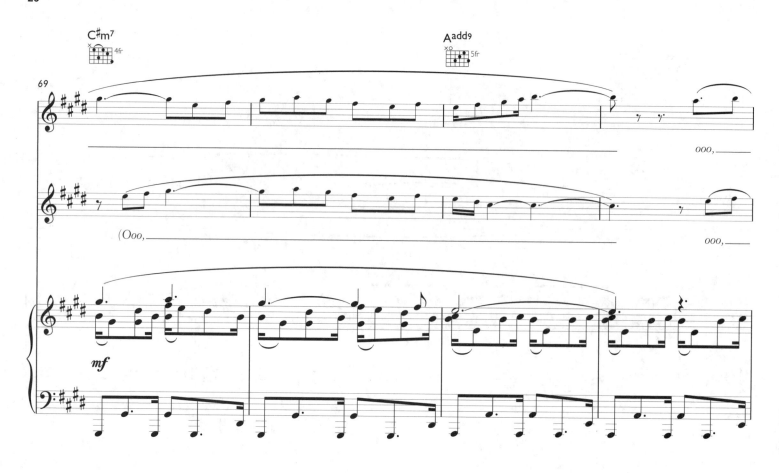

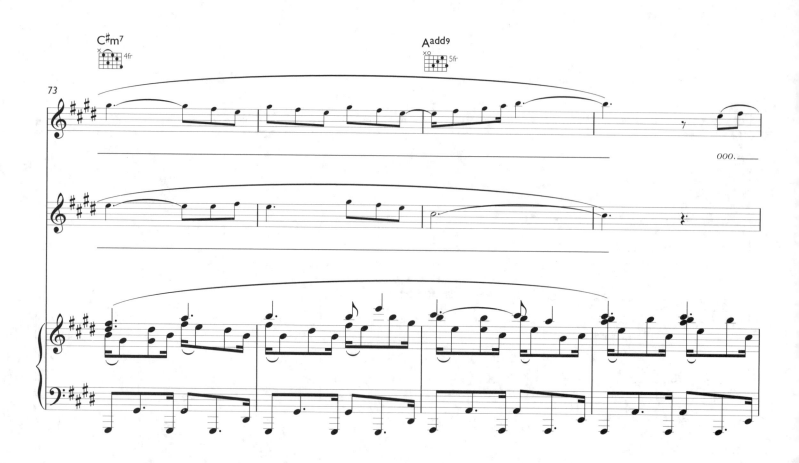

WEIRD FISHES/ARPEGGI

Words and Music by Thomas Yorke, Jonathan Greenwood,
Colin Greenwood, Edward O'Brien and Philip Selway

ALL I NEED

Words and Music by Thomas Yorke, Jonathan Greenwood,
Colin Greenwood, Edward O'Brien and Philip Selway

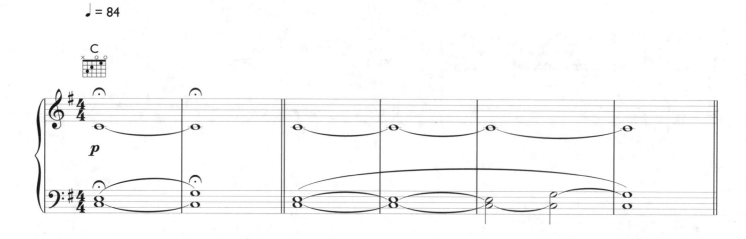

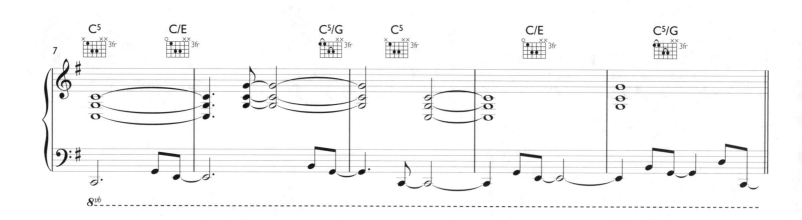

1. I'm the next act, waiting in the wings,
2. I am a moth who just wants to share your light,

(Play small notes 2°)

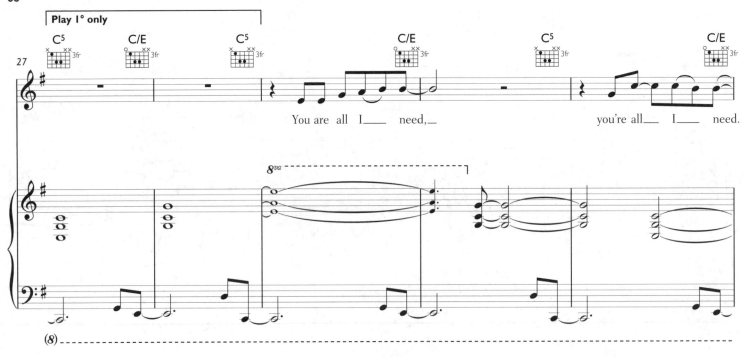

You are all I___ need,___ you're all___ I___ need.

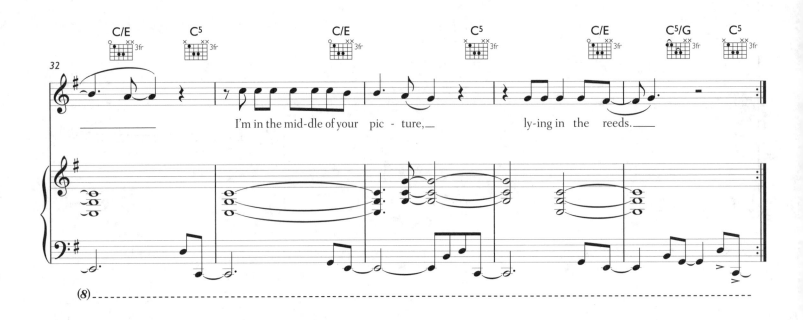

I'm in the mid-dle of your pic - ture,___ ly-ing in the reeds.___

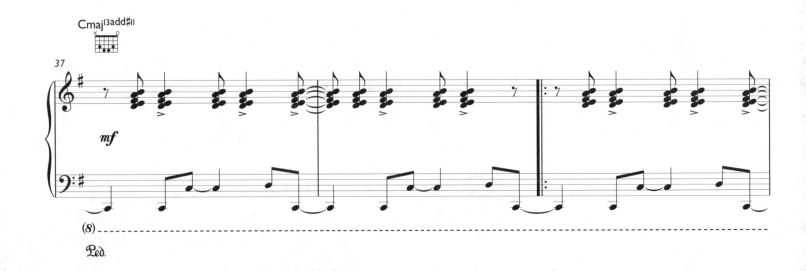

FAUST ARP

Words and Music by Thomas Yorke, Jonathan Greenwood,
Colin Greenwood, Edward O'Brien and Philip Selway

One, two, three, four...

1. Wak - ey, wak - ey, rise and shine, it's on a - gain,___ off a - gain,___
2. Squeeze the tubes___ and emp - ty bot - tles, I take a bow,___ take a bow,___

on a - gain,___ watch me fall___ like dom - in - oes___ in pret - ty pat - terns,
take a bow, it's what you feel___ not what you ought___ to, what you ought___ to. The

You'll go to Hell

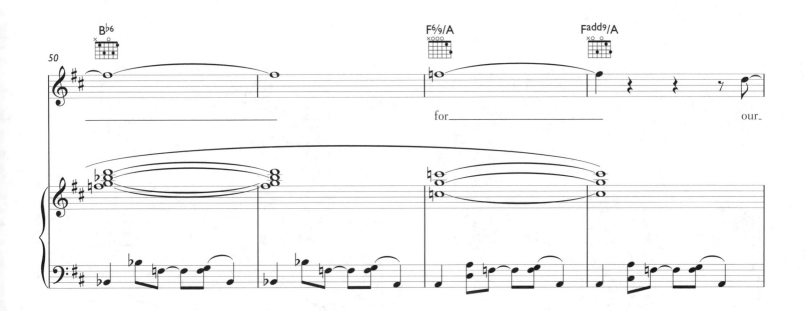

for our

fath-ers. You got melt-

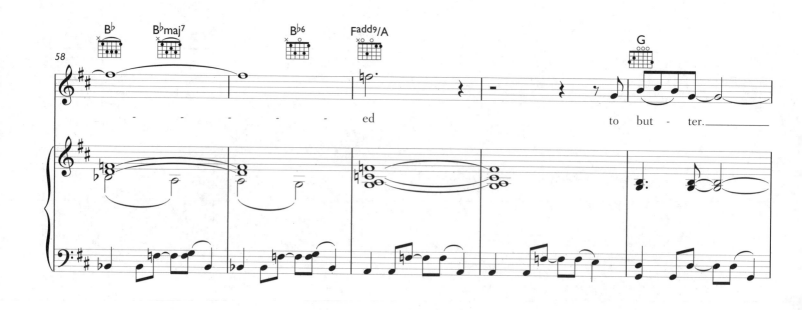

- - - - - ed   to but - ter._____

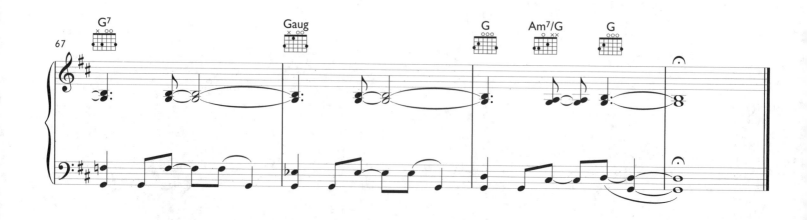

RECKONER

Words and Music by Thomas Yorke, Jonathan Greenwood,
Colin Greenwood, Edward O'Brien and Philip Selway

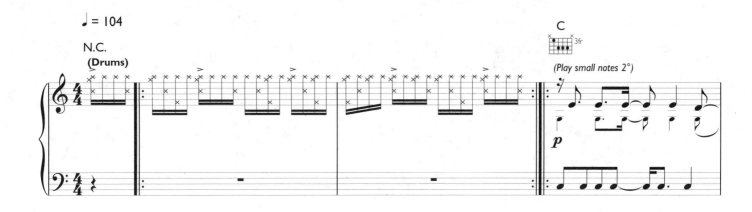

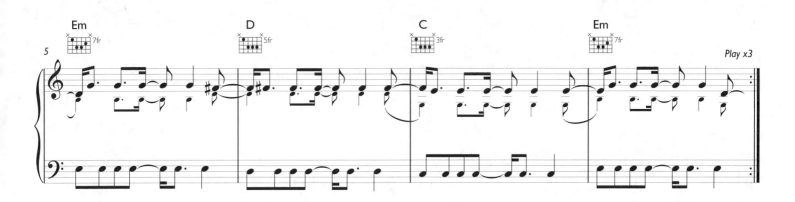

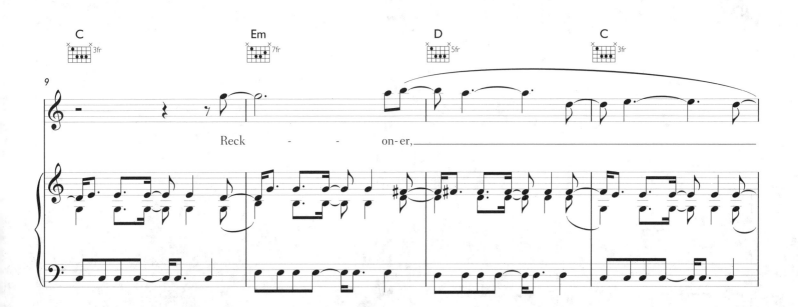

Reck - - on-er,

take_____ me with_____ yer.__

Ded - - i - ca-

- ted___ to___ all_____ hu..._____ all_____ hu -

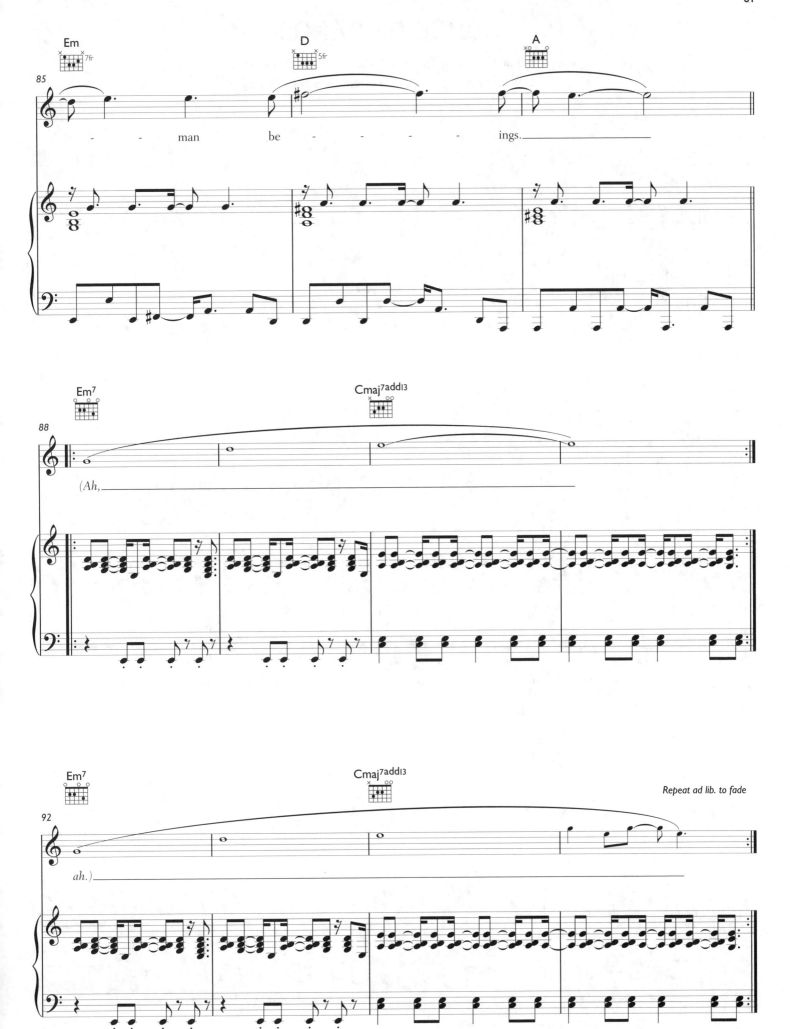

HOUSE OF CARDS

Words and Music by Thomas Yorke, Jonathan Greenwood,
Colin Greenwood, Edward O'Brien and Philip Selway

1. I don't want to be your friend,___ I just want to be your lov -
(2.) in - fra - struc - ture will col - lapse,___ from vol - - tage___ spikes.

- er.

No

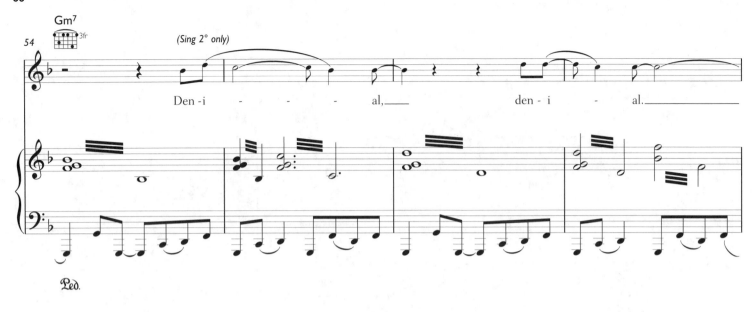

Gm7

54

(Sing 2° only)

Den - i - - al,___ den - i - al.___

Ped.

Fadd9

58

Ped. Ped.

1.

Gm7

62

Den - i - - al,___ den - i - al.___

Ped.

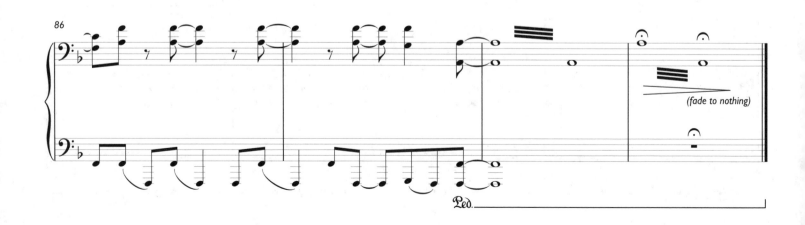

JIGSAW FALLING INTO PLACE

Words and Music by Thomas Yorke, Jonathan Greenwood,
Colin Greenwood, Edward O'Brien and Philip Selway

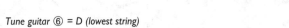

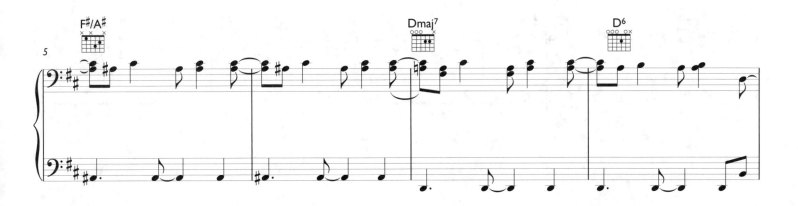

1. (tacet)

Just as___ you take___ my___ hand, just as___ you write___ my___ num-ber down,
The walls are bend - ing___ shape, you got___ a Chesh - ire cat___ grin,___
𝄋 Before you run a - way___ from me,___ before you're lost be - tween___ the notes,___
Come on___ and let___ it___ out,___ come on___ and let___ it___ out,___

(On 𝄋 sing 8va higher)

Mmm,_

mmm,

⊕ **Coda**

dance,   dance,_   dance,   dance,   dance,   dance,_   dance,   dance...

(fade to nothing)

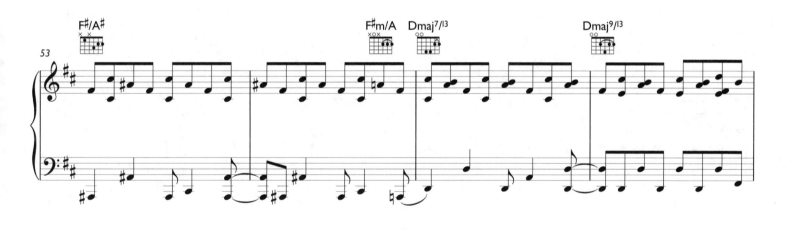

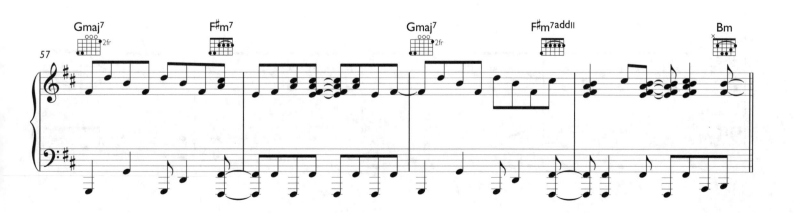

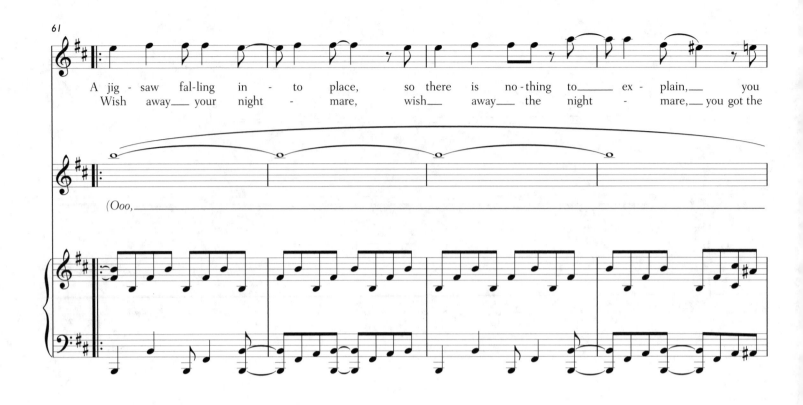

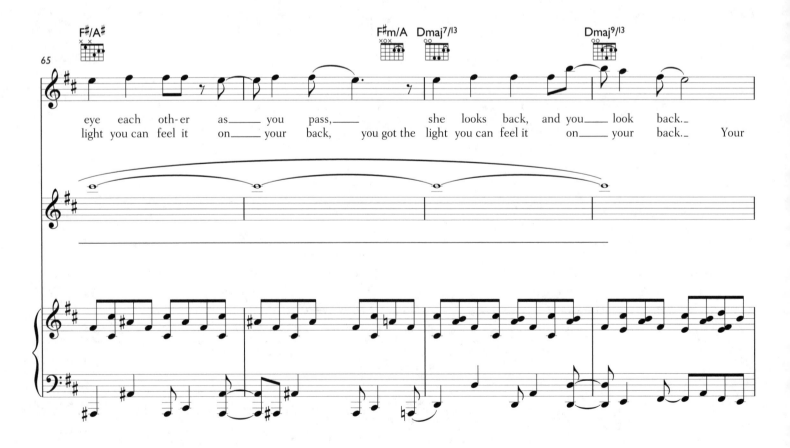

VIDEOTAPE

Words and Music by Thomas Yorke, Jonathan Greenwood,
Colin Greenwood, Edward O'Brien and Philip Selway

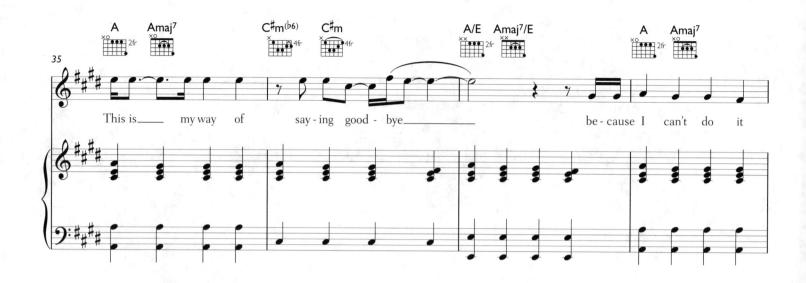

This is___ my way of say - ing good - bye___ be - cause I can't do it

face to face. I'm talk - ing to you be - fore... No mat - ter___ what hap - pens now, you

should-n't be___ a - fraid___ be - cause I know to - day has been the most

per - fect day I have ev - er seen.